# A Saint With A Past…
# But God

*CaLisha White*

# A Saint With A Past

Copyright © 2015 CaLisha White

All rights reserved.

ISBN: 098641090X
ISBN-13: 978-0-9864109-0-1

# A Saint With A Past

THIS BOOK BELONGS TO

_____

FROM:
EVANGELIST CALISHA WHITE
GOD LOVES YOU AND SO DO I XOXO

# A Saint With A Past

## FOREWORD

This book is a must read and amazing testament of the resolve of an amazing woman who defied the odds, overcame the stigma associated with a troubled past by the grace of God. CaLisha White shares intimate and personal experiences of her past. Not for the purpose of earning sympathy or pity, but to help others along the way who may be struggling to overcome the challenges associated with rape, incest, domestic violence, dysfunctional childhood, social exclusion, and various struggles that women face when challenged with overcoming a vicious cycle of adversity. She delivers real talk from someone who can relate to your circumstances and offer you proven solutions because she has walked in many of your shoes. CaLisha White lived a life that packaged so many traumas in one soul since the age of 7. Never been under a doctor's care or received psychiatric treatment or any type of antidepressant to deal with her pain speaks volumes in itself. (This is not an alternative that denounces the use of medicine or disapproval for many to seek medical treatment which in many cases are deemed necessary). It shares struggles and life lessons of a saint who lives life today liberated from a past that many people who suffered similar experiences may still find themselves struggling with I am amazed at her ability to face life head-on everyday with an amazing smile and ability to touch the lives of so many with her compassion and concern for the wellbeing of others and at the same time be an outstanding wife. It is such an honor that God would pair us for reasons greater than our love for each other, but most important for the sake of the ministry. Pray this book blesses your soul!

# A Saint With A Past

## DEDICATION

I would like to dedicate this book to two people...one is my late grandmother, and the other my humble husband.

I dedicate to my late grandmother Gustava Kelly. I am so appreciative of the seed she planted in me about Jesus, when I was seven years old. "One plants, one waters and God will give the increase" -And glory be to God, He did. I love you & I miss you dearly.

I dedicate this book to my husband Curtis White. I thank God every day for you. Through your wisdom and skillful hand, you educated me how to recapture hope back in humanity. I am forever blessed as a woman to grasp what it truly means to "cover" your wife. I love you so much!

# A Saint With A Past

## ACKNOWLEDGMENTS

***I am a firm believer in given people their flowers while they are yet alive:***

- I first want to give thanks to God, who is truly, truly the head of my life. He is the one that I depend on, lean on and reverence. Thank you for blessing me with a gift that I will only use to glorify you. Thank you God for reviving me and allowing me to birth what you have given me so long ago. Thank you for your mercy & grace!

- To my Man of God Elder Curtis White, where do I begin…our love story was not written nor was it rehearsed one thing for sure, it is as real as the blood that pumps through my veins. I am grateful to God that He blessed me with a covering and a man that loves me as I am. Your love for God gave me hope again in humanity and I just want to take the time to tell you I love you and I am blessed to be your wife. Baby thank you for being my covering, my husband, my teacher, my manager, for being my very best friend. You did an amazing job on my book cover & editing, a hidden talent you didn't even know you had xoxo I love you so much!

- I want to always give thanks to my dad and mom {Michael and Linda Glover} for life and for showing me that the "old" can truly learn from the "young".

- I want to thank God for my son DeVante' no matter the mistake or choices you have made in life one thing is for certain, you have always been a great son to me, and I am blessed to be your mother. I love you unconditional always!

- I want to also give a shout out to my other son Dahmel, "thank you" for seeing me as I am & allowing me to love you & be your step-mother.

# A Saint With A Past

- I want to thank ALL my sisters in Christ who have stepped in the gap with me throughout the years: Tiffany Streat, Pastor Shon Hemphill, Prophetess Tamika Brown, Deanna Blackburn, Regina Smith, Penny Clark, Tanya Young, Shaneda Ford, Tonia Stovall, Debbie Oblitas

- Last but not least to ALL my naysayers, fault finders and haters. I want to say **"thank you"**! My haters have truly been my motivators & I say with a sincere heart, "Won't God do it...? Yes He will!" {smile}

# A Saint With A Past

## CONTENTS

- ✓ Introduction..............................
- ✓ Pain taught me obedience..................
- ✓ His mercy & grace covered me.........
- ✓ My pain produced power..................
- ✓ Damaged but not destroyed...............
- ✓ He is my provider..........................
- ✓ Different paths of pain..................
- ✓ My back is strong enough.................
- ✓ There's a story behind this glory.........
- ✓ Poem "A Saint with a Past"...............

# A Saint With A Past

*EVERY SAINT HAS A PAST & EVERY SINNER HAS A FUTURE*

AUTHOR: UNKNOWN

# A Saint With A Past

## Introduction

God knows I am humble and in awe with the gift to write what He has given me. I know often times we say we are not worthy. I would like to say God thank You for finding me worthy. A Saint with a past is a book I feel many of us will be able to relate to. I try to tell people I have not always been on the mountain top, but it was actually in my valley where God made and molded me. God taught me how to not only press but trust. There were times when I felt like my back was literally up against the wall, but I learned it was in those moments that God was holding me up. God has given me the faith that He can do anything but fail. I was hesitant at first to do this book because I wanted to write like most writers and have characters, I didn't want to always be the main character. God let me know people are looking for people to be authentic and someone they themselves can relate to. My prayer is that we always remember where we came from and stay in a place of humility, and at the same time rise from the long suffering and struggles life has brought our way. This book is to remind us of not only where we have been, but also where we're going in God. To stop putting yourself down because of your past, and to remember if God brought you to it, He will see you through it. I believe Donnie McClurkin said it best when he said "A Saint is just a sinner who fell down". That is me and many of you reading this. We give our life to God but every now and then He brings to our remembrance the things He's delivered us from. I am a woman of God who has endured molestation, incest, rape, a child out of wedlock, and cruelty by men, miscarriages, and cast down and excluded by the church, even cervical cancer thought it wanted to knock on my door but I did not answer, and so much more. Even though all those things happened I still have my "joy". Jesus has already won every battle I would ever undergo. My prayer is that you will permit yourself to know you too can suffer and come out on the other side as victorious in spite of your story. It's one thing to speak about it; but when you have truly lived it, you can give people something to not only relate to, but show them that if God did it for me, He most certainly can do it for you. Yes, life is often not fair and neither are people.

# A Saint With A Past

And yes occasionally bad things really do happen to good people. Yet we have a Father who sits up high and looks down low and He knows early rising and our going down in the same. It is only by the **grace** of God that I have lasted; and because you are reading this I truly believe there is hope for you also, to overcome your past and live the life God intended for you to live.

Blessings,
Evangelist CaLisha White

# A Saint With A Past

## PAIN TAUGHT ME OBEDIENCE

**Hebrews 5:8**
*Though he were a Son, yet learned
he obedience by the things which he suffered.*

I am sure many of you reading this can relate to pain. And I am not talking about the pain you feel when you hit your funny bone. I am referring to that deep hidden pain that you try your hardest to not let anyone close to, the pain that you carried out of shame for so long, while longing for some type of relief. The pain of domestic violence and abuse contributed by the hands of someone who says they love you. I am referring to the pain that comes from a broken heart, disappointment, or those times when you felt neglected from a love one. That is the pain which I am speaking about. How comforting is it when God gives us a scripture that can shed a little light on our afflictions? The scripture says, "Jesus learned obedience, by the things which He suffered." If Jesus can learn obedience by which He suffered, surely you and I can as well.

I did not always understand why I had to endure so much pain in life, but one thing is for certain, no matter the size or amount of pain I had encountered in life, it made me want to obey and follow God even the more. The more pain I encountered in life, the closer I wanted to be to God. That is the amazing thing when I chose to give my life to Christ at the tender age of seven. Even when I disobeyed the Holy Ghost, on the inside I would always be convicted and ask God for forgiveness. When you are obedient you are submissive to God. You conform to the ways of Christ.

The Bible says obedience is better than sacrifice. When we sacrifice we are giving up our will for the things we would rather do or want to do in order for us to please the Father. Jesus came down from heaven in the form of a servant and was

# A Saint With A Past

made in the likeness of man. And being found in fashion as a man, he humbled himself, and became obedient unto death, even the death of the cross. {Philippians 2:7,8}. He felt all the pain that we feel and so much more, yet He remained obedient to God. Though people talked about Him, spat on Him, lied on Him, even his own disciple Judas betrayed Him; Jesus suffered the pain and obeyed the calling for His life even in His last hour.

It was not until I typed this that I really got it, the things in which I endured in life had nothing to do with me. It was so much bigger than CaLisha. If you are not careful you will find yourself jumping on that wagon of murmuring and complaining that you may very well miss your witness. **Isaiah 6:8** says, *"Also I heard the voice of the Lord, saying, Whom shall I send, and who will go for us? Then said I, "Here am I; send me."*

That very scripture is what I said to God. "Send me Lord I'll go, I'll tell them rather they want to hear in season or out of season". I have not done anything in life worthy of thee, and to see the revelation unfold right before my eyes I know you are a true and living God. My grief is so that I could minister and witness to someone else going through something similar to what I have gone through. Often times we will be the only Bible that many in this life will ever read. What is your life reading?

So many people ask me how come I am not hostile or livid of the things that took place in my life. I am human; I put my clothes on one leg at a time like everyone else. Yes there were times I remember being livid and hurt, however being bitter has never been an option for me. I chose to ponder on the scripture **{Job 13:15}** *"Though He slay me, yet will I trust in him: but I will maintain mine own ways before Him.* Job here is expressing the unquenchable faith of one who lives by faith, not by sight. Even when it appears that God Himself has turned

# A Saint With A Past

against Job, he still trusted God. Yes there were times in my life where I could not feel His presence. No matter the degree of pain I was encountering I would always say, "my soul still says yes"! My life is not my own, it was bought with a price of Christ's precious blood. I have devoted everything I am and everything I will ever be to the ministry of Christ. I am an Ambassador for Christ.

Only an omnipotent God can take the pain associated with the afflictions we suffer, and with the same pain use it as a teaching tool to reveal to us His will, and an inner strength we have to endure and overcome trials we never would have imagined. Pain taught me how to obey God, and also that I am more than a conqueror. Yes pause for a moment and try to appreciate that, see this is a clear illustration that His ways are not our ways and His thoughts are not our thoughts. Who would have thought that "pain" would be my life lesson?

When you are being taught something it comes with a purpose of imparting, educating, training and the initiating of a memorable experience. In my case my learning would come greatly through memorable experiences associated with pain, and a lot of it. Pain was assigned to teach me how to obey no matter the magnitude of the circumstances I would face in this life. My personal testimony is not for pity, it is to share with others that we all go through things in life, and some more than others, but it is not for naught. Where many of us fall short, is that we are so focused on the hurt caused by pain to our mental and physical state, that we miss out on the opportunity to learn a crucial life lesson that can only be revealed by knowing the will of a loving God that speaks to your spiritual state. This is definitely where I struggled for more than half of my life. It was not until the revelation of this scripture came to pass, that I received a break through and relief for my soul, from years of buildup and torment that I nurtured and entertained for all these years on my own. It is not because

# A Saint With A Past

God was not speaking that it took so long for me to get it, it was because I was in my own way focused on my pain instead of what God was trying to show me. What is God telling you about you through your pain?

My prayer is that someone reading this right now will get the same revelation in which God gave me. Allow your pain to teach you obedience even while reading this book. Everything we go through in life has a season and a purpose. Ask God to reveal yours to you right now

*Dear God,*
*Thank you for giving me the revelation on why you allowed me to suffer. I do know now it has never been about me, but you getting the glory in my life for not only saving me but bringing me out. My prayer is that whoever may be reading this right now may be touched like you touched me, to know we not only have purpose to be about our Fathers Business no matter the cost, but you have already given us the tools we need to proceed. I pray that all men and women learn that in order to truly prosper and be right with God, it takes obedience to His Holy Word, Holy Spirit teach us obedience from the things we have already suffered and the things we will suffer in this life in Jesus sweet name, we pray AMEN*

# A Saint With A Past

## MERCY & GRACE COVERED ME

**Hebrews 8:12**
*For I will be merciful toward their iniquities,
and I will remember their sins no more."*

If it was not for God's mercy and grace I would not be able to get out of bed every morning. I am so serious when I type that statement. It is because of God's mercy, grace and unwavering love that give me not only a reason but strength to go on every day. What a lot of people don't know is just because you have a calling on your life and you answer the call to God does not mean life is not still difficult, or that you may fall into sin. What it means is you can go through this problematical life with Jesus, & no matter how difficult or trying this world may be, having confidence in knowing that God stills bestow His mercy & grace is far more rewarding then any silver or gold.

Permit me to share where Gods mercy and grace showed up tremendously in my life. I was in a relationship where I lost who I was as a woman. I had been physical and mental abused for so many years by my ex-husband and even when he stopped putting his hands on me physically the abuse that I was receiving mentally messed me up for a long time. I could not understand why this was happening to me. Well maybe that's not true, I saw all the signs before I got married to this man, he was cheating, lying, and beating on me when we was courting, and my self-esteem was so low I truly believed I was getting what I deserved.

 I recall him telling me I was a used up woman and no man would ever want to be with me because of my past rapes. When you hear something like that you entertain the idea that it could very well be true. So I stayed and I put on a mask for so long, and even in the house of God no one had a clue at what this woman of God was going through. I learned at an early age how to not show what was really going on in my home. I had reached a point in my life where I had a nervous breakdown, I truly lost my mind and when I tried to take my own life it was Gods mercy and grace that showed up for me. And God said I shall live and not die.

# A Saint With A Past

How do I do it God? How do I continue on in this marriage where I want to end my own life? I was too ashamed to tell my family what was really going on, because many family members placed bets on how long my marriage would last, can you believe blood could do something so cruel?

I didn't have anywhere else to go; it was just me and my son that was my family. I had left home when I was 17 going on 18. What do you do when you have nowhere else to go, and the place where your living is a living h*ll? Although I was an Evangelist, I was also a damaged woman. The church saw the anointing on my life but seemed only interested that I teach their women, and preach to their congregations. But how come these same people of God could not discern my broken heart?

I had truly given up on life and lost all hope in humanity. I thought my childhood was one engulfed with catastrophic circumstances, but my first two marriages were as well. I shared with these men the abuses I had already suffered in life. Why in God's name would they want to add to it instead of helping me? I did something that I am not proud of, something as a woman I thought I never would do, especially since respect and integrity are high on my list.

It was God's mercy and grace that covered me when I had an affair. What! The Evangelist had an affair. Yes! This saved, sanctified, filled with the Holy Ghost woman of God had an affair when I was married to my ex – husband. It is not something that I'm pleased of, nor do I excuse. Adultery is a sin; whether you do it physically or entertain an emotional affair it is all sin. So is judging, so if you are while you are reading this please beloved, please **STOP**! And never ever say what you will and will not do, never think that certain things in life cannot happen to you, because it can. I am a living witness.

I can recall before the affair how I would minister to so many men and women of God that found themselves in similar situations, and although I did not judge, I found it hard to comprehend how something like that could happen to you, particularly if you were saved. I prayed for them, I

# A Saint With A Past

ministered and spoke life into them, and many reading this are the ones I ministered to.

When I found myself in that same dilemma, when I needed mercy and grace, prayer, and just a little compassion from those especially who labored with me and knew my character and heart, very few extended it. I was shunned from the church, so called friends stop dealing with me. Many who "pretended" to be my friends stuck around long enough to see me hit rock bottom. It was as though people were waiting and almost glad to see that I also am fallible, and human. I was crying from a deep place and nobody heard me, or cared. They turned their backs on me and the pain was great, because I loved them and thought they loved me.

Now I don't know what the exact protocol was for having an affair so this is what I did. I first repented to God. I repented to my ex-husband; I repented to the woman whose husband I was having the affair with. I repented to the church. I sat down for three years. And I was still judged, shunned, name ran through the mud. Unfortunately the torment wouldn't stop there.

My actions had consequences, and to whom much is given much is required. But my son almost losing his life shook me to the very depths of my soul; the thought of losing him was too much to bear. It was one thing to lose the respect of my name and have my character questioned, and to lose so many close friends, but my son was my pride and joy who gave me so much reason at a dark time in my life to live. To put the knife a little deeper in my heart, a pastor allowed his flesh to rise and speak in the pulpit that I am getting what I deserve because of what I did. How does one digest that comment let alone understand it?

You truly have to be a mother to understand the pain that accompanies the news of hearing that your only birthed child was shot in the chest ½ inch from his heart, with the bullet piercing his lung, and blowing out ½ of his stomach and hitting his pancreas. I was told by the doctors that they had lost him once, and he was not breathing on his own they had to put him on a respirator and said he slipped into a coma. He was diagnosed

# A Saint With A Past

with a 10% chance of living, and if recovered his life would be met with debilitating medical issues due to the extent of his injuries.

I was more than 5000 miles away when I received the devastating news, can you imagine the plane ride. I needed to hear from God. I could not lose my son, not this way Lord! Then the Holy Ghost said, "Look at your ticket"! As my eyes looked down at my ticket my eyes began to tear up. My seat ticket was 33D my! my! my! allow me a moment to praise God!!!!! No matter how much I have done, no matter how many mistakes one can make, I am certain that Gods love is real. He reassured me in my time of need that in spite of everything, He still had hands on me. The reason why that number is so significant is because when DeVante my son played football his jersey number was 33 and I called him "D short" for DeVante'. When I sat down in that seat, God gave me an overwhelming peace that rested on me the whole flight, and I knew everything was going to be alright.

When I finally reached my son, and seen the tubes protruding from all over his body, and his face covered by the oxygen mask, and the sound of the various machines that was keeping him alive. I was shaken for a moment, but what mother wouldn't be. But the peace of God revived me, and I said God please show your mercy and grace in this situation, please show favor unto your servant. You said you have given me hands of healing Lord, allow me to lay hands on my son and let him live and not die. My faith to lay hands on him by the unction of the Holy Ghost was activated and he opened his eyes. Doctors said it was a miracle; But God. It was only by Gods mercy and grace that I am able to say that God healed him and he rose up from his bed of affliction after 3 months, 100% recovered.

It crossed my mind that maybe what happened to my son was a consequence of a choice I made, and sadly I began to fall into this fleshly way of thinking because that is what was being preached across so many church pulpits I was told, and among the many associates who was privy to my situation. But that's not the God I serve, He is a forgiving God, and I'm thankful He's not like man, to hold grudges. It doesn't take that much

# A Saint With A Past

to shake me right, when I'm wrong. I repented of my sins and asked for forgiveness, and He proved me by sparing my sons life that I am forgiven. Could you imagine if God was to take a child for every adulterous affair in the church, there wouldn't be many firstborns living today?

Now my son chose to hang around a certain crowd and it almost cost him his life, he is of age, and I turned him over to God a long time ago, but I'm grateful that the pain of this situation taught me about the mercy of God, and to tell you today, to not allow people, or a wrong choice to keep you hostage from experiencing the love of God. Repent of your sins and know that God is not holding whatever that thing is over your head, if God be for us; He is more than the world against us.

Isn't it sad at how so many would gravitate to your faults and shortcomings, and show very little remembrance of the things you done right? Yes having that affair cost me my credibility, banishment from the church, no one would minister to me but rather excommunicated me as a leper. How could this be? Many have issues because I am on my third marriage; yes you read it right 1, 2, and 3! When I made my first two choices in marriage it was definitely out of my flesh, I did not consult God about anything. My last and final marriage I did. I went before God before I said I do. When we don't wait on God and we go in our own way you take the chance of missing the mark.

My choice in men cost me a lot in my past marriages. I was a woman who survived physical and emotional abuse that spanned 18 years. My previous relationships were toxin and abusive and I stayed because I did not know I had self-worth until God revealed it to me in 2011. I saw a lot of red flags yet I still proceeded, and not with caution. And just like I chose to stay I also had the same choice to leave. The troubling thing about my story is that I had so many people who chose rather to distant themselves from me when I finally got into a marriage that God envisioned for me from the beginning. With some people anything that is unorthodox they feel is wrong.

# A Saint With A Past

One thing I have learned a long time ago is that you don't have to put no one on display for their wrong doing. God has a way of taking care of His children and those who mishandle them, often times when people receive their just recompense for acts they commit you may know nothing about it. I am yet still reminded about how His mercy and grace covered me, and I ask God to have mercy on those who have abused their authority.

I was a woman who really wanted to be loved ever since I was a little girl, I wanted to belong. When you don't have self-confidence or the privilege of a safety net resulting from an environment that deprived you of love and acceptance as a child, especially when you're a little girl, you will grab a hold of the first thing that gives you a fairytale expression of genuine love, when really it's a facade. I will admit I was a naïve woman. I thought I could change a man to be loving, kind, and faithful, but twice I was wrong. See I had to learn that change not only comes from within, it comes from God. Unless God converts the heart "you" will never be able to keep a man with the comfort of peace in your heart. Many times we find ourselves being deceitful, calculating, and devious in our actions in trying to change a person to be what we want them to be, and it just doesn't work like that, trust me! I'm not telling you what I heard; I'm telling you what I know. Through it all God as covered me from the time I was formed in my mother's womb. I have had a lot of suffering in my lifetime; so many reasons to give up, but through it all God saw fit to shower me with His mercy and grace and I will always be humble and thankful. God's mercy and grace gave me another chance at life and He blessed me with my husband, Curtis. It was through his love that I regained hope back again in humanity and I knew God has forgiven me and was blessing me to truly be loved and accepted, being seen through the eyes of a man for the first time seeing me for who I really am. It is truly worth the wait, when you wait on God.

Friends, Beloved, Saints of God; true mercy is showing compassion, forgiveness, kindness and sympathy. Possessions we will all need one day to whether our own personal storms. When you show someone compassion, your own intellect should not come in place, a sincere concern of someone else feelings and state of mind does. Never say what

# A Saint With A Past

can and cannot happen to you. I said, "I would never stay with a man if he puts his hands on me. I also said, "I would never be unfaithful" and I did even though I had a desire to never do any of them. By default we a can be faultfinders we have to remember we all are fallible and could very well "fall from grace". And many of you reading this did and are so grateful to God that not only did He not expose you, He poured out His mercy and grace on you and this is why you show others love and compassion, not judgment and condemnation.

It is only God's mercy that allows me to show mercy towards others. That's why I was able to forgive **all** my abusers, the ones who abused me sexually, and the ones who abused me physically. Abuse is not always sexual or physical; abuse can also be the malicious psychological abuse of the mind. I was able to pardon everyone not just my exes or the men who raped me, but all the men and women in my life that abused their authority. Besides what would that say about the God I confess lives in me, if I was not able to transform my pain and circumstances to an opportunity to glorify God through seeing someone else through their pain? Just like pain is felt when giving birth to a child, it is long forgotten after the joy of receiving a healthy child. What joy is attached to your pain? Trust me; there is a reason that spells victory for you when you diligently seek Him for your purpose.

Many of you reading this right now have been malicious, angry, mean, bitter, and belligerent to someone who has truly wronged you and probably never made that wrong right. Why not do it now? Even if you can't contact them you can ask God to forgive you for your short comings with those individuals. We all will go through storms and mercy is something we definitely want others to convey to us. I say it all the time, half the people that hurt you doesn't know, and the other half doesn't care.

# A Saint With A Past

*Dear God, I thank You for being the Alpha and the Omega in my life the beginning and the end. Thank you for showing us mercy and grace. I thank you that you don't give us the punishment that we ought to receive, and although many tried to play God, I thank you for being the true and living God. Please cover the ones reading this right now with your mercy and grace and let them know truly how necessary it is for us to receive it from You. In Jesus sweet name I pray AMEN*

# A Saint With A Past

## MY PAIN PRODUCED POWER

**Romans 8:28**
*And we know that all things work together
for good to them that love God, to them
who are the called according to his purpose.*

One of my favorite scriptures in the Bible is Romans 8:28; *"All things work together for good to them that love God, to them who are the called according to His purpose".* When you meditate on that scripture, you are able to see that the thing that was purposed for bad in your life is an opportunity for a good outcome according to a Godly purpose. I thank God for the opportunity to take every rape; every domestic beating; incest; cancer; losing my mind; rejection by family and friends; loneliness; depression; every heart ache I ever experienced along this suffering way, and use it for an opportunity to use me to be useful and pleasing to Him. My pain taught me how to endure, how to persevere, how to truly depend on God. Not just when things are difficult do I turn to Him, but when things are good as well.

We have to learn that the enemy is not going to give us a break, he's the devil, and evil is never nice. There is something that the enemy wanted to destroy in me from the womb, no other explanation can explain the senseless and momentous suffering and trials I faced in my life, people just don't like me without cause, and if you're not careful you would think that your cursed, but I am here to tell you that your blessed, your blessed when men shall revile you, and persecute you, and say all manner of evil against you falsely for my name sake, for great is your reward in heaven saith the Lord in "Matthew 5:11". Let your pain, be an opportunity for gain in God. Let Him show you that He loves you and understands. He has made a way of escape for every doubt in your mind concerning the many daunting circumstances in your life that's connected to His purpose working for the good.

My pain created resilience inside, no matter what has happened in my life God has always let me bounce back and for every time I had to bounce

# A Saint With A Past

back my comeback was greater than the one before. That's why this book is so special to me, in every single testimony I will express a temporary setback, and then you will read how Great God has been in my life and allowed me to come out on the winning side every time. Everything that happens in our lives is not by chance, through all of the injustice that came my way; God is still the ultimate Judge. (He sees all and knows all).

I could not understand for the life of me why I was so excluded and rejected of women. {Not all women but a good majority of them}. Whether in the house of God, at work, school, with in laws, and sad to say even among members of my own family the results are the same, " drama". I don't know what it's like to experience a true sisterhood, and I longed for it. I have no sisters, and for so long, longed to have another woman I can simply have girl talk with, just to share those things women speak about, and to have another woman to bounce things off, intimate things that women face to see if I'm on or off track. For a time especially coming up in the church I had no older women who would entreat me as a daughter and show me the ropes, everything I learned concerning being a woman, I learned from God. He instructed me in how to walk in heels, how to talk intelligently, proper edict and how to conduct myself with class, and for that I'm truly grateful to Him. I'm human I still have feelings that we all experience one time or another. To not have such a simple luxury that women are capable of giving, definitely has been a travesty by far, a longing I ultimately turned over to God.

I observed through the years that the reason there's tension and distance between a lot women is because **"that in which you lack you often attack"**. I had to really examine this a little closer but from a spiritual perspective. Many times people just want to be ugly because they have been able to do so, and not be held accountable by being confronted and disciplined accordingly. And there are those who are just down right evil, and there's nothing you can do about it but pray for them. Before I got saved and addressed matters according to the flesh, I found myself fighting jealous women all the time from middle school all the way through college. I would get propositioned to fight for the most trivial reasons. I realized that this cycle of violence was never going to change from my

# A Saint With A Past

hope of women wising up and realizing I mean no harm as a result of the way God made me.

I had a paradigm shift. The unexplainable and unwanted friction I would encounter throughout my life could only be a calling and anointing on my life I myself was not aware of. This was about something greater than me, and me believing that the calamity surrounding my life was based on the notion that I was the best thing God ever made. There is something special about me and my failure to seek God for understanding would continue this vicious cycle of negative aggression with my sisters. When God revealed to me that I would be set apart for the work of the ministry to minister to women in matters of holiness, my understanding flooded with confirmation to the countless friction I encountered throughout the years with women that I could give no reasonable explanation for. I understand now my purpose.

I am now learning how to fight everyday with the word of God, and not my own words, and for me it is a daily feeding because this habit of speaking my mind was second nature, and only God can address the matter of my tongue. My husband who also witnessed my issues with women encourages me to remember that Jesus told us *that if the world hates you, know that they first hated Him, and that a prophet is not without honor, but in his own country, and among his own kin, and in his own house.* So what I'm facing is not uncommon for those who must live the difference of what's holy and unholy, and when you choose to live according to a standard, it is often met with opposition, so I receive my calling.

So if the pain of a troubled childhood, being abused by men, and the rejection of the church was not enough, I had to also endure the pain of being rejected and misunderstood by women. This is where my pain produce power comes in; I chose to use the pain I was carrying and turn it into something good. I made a choice to be happy, I chose to love, and I chose to forgive. I chose to answer my call and watch God birth a great ministry out of me for hurting women. I didn't want to be like many and lose control or become a bad influence because of the things that

# A Saint With A Past

happened to me. I didn't feel justified to be cruel, nasty, and mean to people just because I had it rough, instead I chose to flip it.

My pain, my hurt, my sorrow, my rejection, all this pressure caused a birthing to take place in the spirit, and what God allowed me to birth He also allowed me to nurture. Hold on while I shout on that one. See you have to understand my pain produced power from within. My prayer is that anyone reading this right now will get that broken heart healed starting now, and while you are waiting you give no more power over to the devil that you chose to grasp how your response is going to be, rather life is fair or not. You will not allow the enemy to take the power God has placed inside of you.

*Dear Lord I ask that you touch the person reading this right now and give them strength to stand in spite of all that they have been through and the pain they have had to carry. I ask that you touch them right now and allow them to feel your love and learn to turn their pain into power, give them the garment of praise for the spirt of heaviness. Let them know we have a choice and tomorrow can be a little lighter, a little sweeter, a little better if we choose to make it that way, it is in Jesus sweet name we pray,*

# A Saint With A Past

## DAMAGED BUT NOT DESTROYED

**Matthew 7:25**
*"And the rain descended and the floods came, and the winds blew, and beat upon that house; and it fell not: for it was founded upon a rock"*

Anyone who has been raped molested, or a victim of incest knows that once a man or woman abuses you sexually it brings with it many debilitating affects both psychologically and physically. It crushes your self-esteem and self-worth; I found it difficult to trust and struggled for years with insecurity. Various times I attempted suicide from the feeling of hopelessness. When people try to kill themselves, they're really saying I am broken, will someone hear my cry, but because the cry comes from within no one can really hear it unless you are in tune with the Spirit of God.

Healing is a process and I will give you the five letter name that healed me "Jesus".... I thought that I would never know what it felt like to make love to a man, or feel like a woman because I had been passed around and tampered with so much. If you never lost your mind tell God thank you, see I know what it feels like to lose your mind, but I am thankful that God gave it back to me and He now is the center of my life. So those who want to know why I shout and cry out to God so much it's because I am thanking Him for life, and I am often reminded that I almost missed the mark. To a person who was walking around in darkness not knowing if they would ever see the light of day, and to now not only see the beauty of a life worth living, but to see the beauty of a soul within I am forever grateful for the grace of God.

I was seven years old when a grown man decided he wanted me to make me a woman and took my virginity. After that it was like a snowball effect, like I had a sign on my head that said "do what you want to me". I literally had all kinds of men molest, and rape me. I never knew what the meaning was to have a first. When I got older and started having relationship with men, I often wondered if asked should I count the ones who raped and

# A Saint With A Past

molested me. It took me awhile but I learned that these men who were really weak and disturbed pedophiles took advantage of me because they could, I was just a baby and did nothing wrong. They not only took my body but they took my power, my self-esteem, my confidence away from me and for a long time I despised them and I wanted nothing more than to get even with them. But I thank God for Jesus...Jesus knew my pain, and He knew how tired I was but He did not allow me to seek retaliation on my own. I can honestly say healing is a process and God has delivered me and He is still healing me from my past. I may not be where I want to be....but I thank God I am not where I use to be.

I was so numb, I didn't know how to make love or what love making really was and God knew to give me my husband , he may not have known all that was in store by asking me to be his wife, but one thing I do know our relationship was a "God thing". I thought being on my back was my duty because that's what men made me feel like for so long. That's why good fathers are so important in a little girl's life. I was so messed up in my own mind that I thought in order for me to relieve some of this pain I needed to cut or kill myself...if it was a shock for you to read it, just imagine how tough it was for me to write it down.

When people try to "commit suicide what their really saying is" Help me". When I use to cut myself it was so that I could release the heaviness and pain that was tormenting me in my mind. As foolish as that sounds I cut myself because I needed to know I was still alive because I couldn't feel. I was also in this frame of mind because I lost my mind. Imagine being young women having to process so much painful outrages in your mind and through it all find a reason to feel good about yourself; it can be too much for any one person to try and handle let alone understand.

I was in a relationship with a man when I was much younger and this man used to beat me, not because I stepped out on him, or the house wasn't clean, or dinner wasn't ready. He beat me because he couldn't fathom my past and instead of helping me by seeking professional help, he made the young woman in me even more petrified. He told me I would never do better than him, that no man would ever want to be with someone like me

# A Saint With A Past

who was all used up. For a long time I believed what he said and I stayed and I endured his abuse. The strange thing is I could handle his physical abuse a lot more than I could his emotional abuse. See when you already have a history of being treated like you aren't anything, you start to believe you really aren't anything. One day instead of him hitting me, he hit my son and that's when I knew it was time for me to go, because had I stayed I would have killed him, because at that time my son was the only reason why I wanted to live. Isn't that something we can have love for someone else, but can't find that same love for our self?

When a woman has been treated so badly for so long it's hard to embrace when you are being treated well. It has always been easy for me to push people away because I was often pushed aside. I was so damaged and so hurt for so long I didn't trust anyone not even myself. I never meant to give anyone power over me, men just took it. But God showed me I was broken but not beyond repair. When you come to God knowing your broken it's a miraculous thing to see Him put you back together again. Sometimes we go through for so long, so that when God restores us we can give nobody but Him the credit. All of us have something that God wants to use as an opportunity to show Himself mighty in your life. The kind of repair I needed could not come through man, only a loving God could have touched the inner most parts of my soul that was so lost in darkness, and resurrect me back to life again where my smile today really reflects the gratitude of finding worthiness in His eyes to live and not die. I'm truly innocent and have nothing to be ashamed about.

God gave me a twelve step process of being free from being sexually abused. The **first step** is **Acknowledge,** to acknowledge means to admit the truth. I had to really admit to myself what happened to me. For so long I was in denial, I pretended like I was ok but if you looked deep into my eyes you could see I wasn't. I had to admit that these men took advantage of me and what they did to me was wrong and it wasn't my fault. So the first step is to acknowledge what has happen to you.

The **second step** is to **Forgive myself**. It took me a long time to do this because for so long I thought it was my fault because I didn't tell anybody

# A Saint With A Past

in the beginning. I felt I allowed them to get away with this. So God showed me I was a child and the things that happen to me was not my fault, and when you are humiliated, or defenseless already you close up without even knowing. I had to forgive myself and not beat myself up for not telling what happened, and not blame myself that I had this repulsive thing happen to me.

I gained so much weight being depressed, and I thought if I make myself unattractive I would not have to worry about another man ever raping me again. I had to forgive CaLisha, see this wasn't just a sexual thing this was also a mental and emotional thing God had to bring me through, how to forgive myself and when you forgive you cease to resent.

The **third step** is to **Forgive them.** Now this one was hard on me because I felt I had a valid reason why I didn't have to forgive. And God let me know I had a reason, but I didn't have any right. I heard Tyler Perry say, "When you forgive someone, you take your power back" and that's exactly what happened.

God then introduced me to Juanita Bynum "No more Sheets". When I saw this sermon…I was not only going through the process of being healed, but I started to get delivered. There's a part where Juanita Bynum says "she had to call back all her private areas from around the world", then it hit me, I had to go before God and call back all my private areas that men had taken from me and then I had to purge myself.

To purge is to cleanse from impurity, bodily, and spiritually. Imagine all the men who had their way with me, had released themselves inside of me, I was walking around with all their toxin inside of me plus the guilt of what they had done to me. God allowed me right in my living room to purge and cry out to Him like never before and I did it for hours, until God said it was done. God had me get a glass of water and put three teaspoon of oil in it {Father, Son, and Holy Ghost} and swallowed it all. I remember He had me go into the shower and in the shower is where I received my spiritual bath and from that day forward I didn't feel like I could smell them or feel them because God had cleanse me inside and out and I didn't have any

# A Saint With A Past

residue of them left on me.

The **fourth step** is <u>**Talking**</u>. Imagine having the guilt and shame of any type of abuse built up inside of you for so long, it was the reason I lost my mind at first. That's too much for anyone to carry alone and although I was developing a relationship with Jesus, I didn't completely know how to cast my burdens upon Him. So I began to talk about it and share my story with others in bits and pieces, but God of course knew everything. I trusted Him not to ever judge me and to always love me.

The more I began to speak about my past, the more I would begin to feel liberated; I could feel the burdens of my pain being lifted off my shoulders. My tears became my medicine because I was releasing and I always tell people, "Tears are liquid prayers that only God can understand". I encourage you to ask God to direct you to whom you can share this with, make sure you seek godly guidance and wisdom from above.

The **fifth step** is <u>**Releasing**</u>...the Webster dictionary defines release as: to set free; I was in bondage for so long about my past that I didn't know how to release any of my pain, and when I did release it was not in the right way. I had to talk to myself as if I was speaking to someone else and tell myself...it was not your fault, you do not have to carry this burden anymore.

See the devil is very tricky and devious, he has studied us for a long time, so every time I spoke it out loud not realizing he was listening he tried to bring it back to my remembrance, and every time was stronger than before. This is why God tells us to renew our mind daily with the Word of God. When you renew your mind daily through prayer and meditating on the Word of God you are having dialogue and intimacy with God make sure that in your exchange of releasing the inner most hurts of your heart, that your also opened for God to pour back into you...this is where I was messing up, I was releasing but I wasn't paying attention to what was being poured back inside of me.

{Many will probably purge on this step as well, if you didn't get it out in

# A Saint With A Past

Step 3}. So make sure when you release you immediately allow God to pour back into your spirit man.

The **six step** is **Deliverance**....To get delivered from something that has had a hold on your life for so long could only be performed by God. When I got delivered I surrendered to God. I had to let go and let God. I could no longer try and make sense of the offenses I suffered. Yes! It doesn't make sense; it was wrong what happened to me and that's a reality I have to accept. "It Happened". No matter how much I wanted to deny it, no matter how many times I went over it in my mind the fact is it happened. When I accepted that reality then I was able to get delivered. Just because you accept something does not mean you agree with it.

When you get delivered you are saying, "God I submit this whole situation to you, and when you submit you obey God, you are no longer trying to figure anything out or make sense of it you learn to accept what has happened and know that in the end that what the devil meant for bad God is going to make it for your good.

When you truly get delivered you are no longer psychologically traumatized by the pain of a traumatic event you initially experienced. Now it does not mean that you will not feel discomfort when these areas are revisited through conversation or times of reflection. It means that the pain overtime no longer has the same debilitating effects that it once had in preventing you from experiencing liberty. It's like a cut on the finger, initially it hurts; it calls for immediate attention to address, you may need to run cold water to clean the wound and apply pressure with a bandage to stop the bleeding. Initially the pain is severe and subsides with care and over time. After a few days you take the bandage off and notice that it's starting to heal on it's on, the skin that was cut is starting to close up, after a little while a scab starts to form. If you make the mistake of removing the scab too soon you will realize that the inside is still tender and the scab was a cover for it while healing. It's a natural process that takes time to heel. God nurtures our pain the same way, He is the doctor, and has the care and remedy to heel your broken heart. The problem for so many of us is that we don't come to Him for deliverance. He is waiting for you.

# A Saint With A Past

For me I knew when God had truly delivered me in certain areas of my life. My pain was once intense when I spoke about the tragedy that happened. The reason the pain was still prevalent at one time was because I was nurturing that pain inside of me. God said give it over to me. This is why I had to educate myself in the deliverance process. Today I can talk openly about my travails and not be ashamed, by this I know I am delivered.

The **seventh step** is **Healing**. You will always hear me say, "Healing is a process" it takes time. Now not to be confused with deliverance, this is being liberated from the grips of the pain that has tormented you because of the guilt or shame of the abuse. It's facing your pain and insecurities head on. After being delivered from bondage it is important that your emptiness now be filled and restored with the Holy Spirit, which leads and guides us in all manner of truth. When you are going through the stage of being healed, God is making you whole, He's restoring you, He's cleansing you, He's repairing you, to make you whole and complete again. Will you always have the memories of what happened to you? Yes. I would be doing really well and then something would trigger my past and I would find myself hurting all over again. The Holy Ghost brings things back to my remembrance concerning the things of God and restores me to a right place. You have to fight negative thoughts with positive ones, and the Holy Ghost helps us bring those thoughts subject to the knowledge of God.

One of the reasons it took me so long to be healed of my sexual abuse was because it was hard to let go. Even though it was something horrible and negative, and a heavy burden it was a part of me and I realized often times I was going through the motions but not holding true substance, and God took me back to the beginning and I had to keep repeating these steps until I received my healing from God. So do not try to fool yourself or anyone else, trust God 100%. This step requires getting into the Word of God regularly and getting to know who He is for you. Find yourself a good bible teaching church that teaches the Word of God.

The **eighth step** is **Longsuffering** is *patience in spite of troubles,*

# A Saint With A Past

*especially those caused by others.* To be longsuffering is to be willing and courageous to face the ridicule, ignorance, and misconceptions of others as your integrated back into your social circle with a new attitude and grip on life. "I don't care what you think about me I'm healed" is my new attitude. Don't be dismayed when you get the funny looks and distance from people when they hear your testimony. I find it to be my greatest tester to expose those who are genuinely for me, and those who are not. One of the greatest gifts that God has given me is patience in this area. When I was going through the process of living with my truth and not being ashamed of it, it's amazing how I didn't find many sympathizer's along the way, but a great part of my healing is helping others with my story and the road sometimes get rough, but it's not for naught, and you have to press on.

This ability is not easy, at first, I was angry, I was upset, I was hurt, and I wanted revenge. But God taught me how to endure and it took spiritual surgery. Now God is my doctor and He already knew exactly where my pain was because He created me. Imagine having open heart surgery, once the doctor performs the surgery he has to sew the area back up and this area is very sensitive and the slightest thing could cause you to slip back into despair. Well the same thing with spiritual surgery, God had done the surgery and now I had to long suffer while I was healing.

The **ninth step** is **Honesty**....sigh why is this so hard for us to do? You have to first be honest with yourself before you can be honest with anyone else. I had to be honest or shall I say truthful on what happened to me. Now in my case I felt my honesty was a curse because at first it seemed like no one believed me. I kept hearing so many people say, there's no way you could have gone through all the things you suffered and function the way you do.

I thought to myself what am I supposed to look like after going through the things I went through? I was seven years old when my purity was taking from me, and from seven to twelve years old a family member had incest with me, and then that same family member charged his friends a dollar each to fondle me. I was raped by a military man when I was thirteen, at

# A Saint With A Past

fifteen a family member had incest with me while I was pregnant with my son, and I was raped at 19 in a park in front of my son who was three years old. For years I suppressed the memories of a lot of my childhood ordeals and I found out that studies show that miraculously, not all children or youth molestation victims display signs that something is wrong. But as the years progressed I began noticing varying emotional effects as a result of my trauma like depression, inability to judge trustworthiness in others, mistrust, and anger. When I tried to enter into a relationship with a young man, I can remember being very uncomfortable when he tried to touch me, I started to have flashbacks and I needed to understand why, I was told by my dad after being raped by a soldier at thirteen I would be ok. I wasn't treated medically or psychologically for any of my trauma; it was something that was swept under the rug not to be spoken about. I guess I was a small matter when compared to the controversy the rape issue would have caused. But somehow at 13, I had to figure out on my own how to live with it. Now at 16, I got to a point I was ready to break my silence and be honest about what happened to me.

When I was honest with my family first the reaction I received was as if I was being raped all over again. No one believed me, they questioned me, they mocked me, and not one put their arms around me and tried to help me through this horrific pain I had been living with for so many years. Support is important, and when you don't receive it, it's basically being told that you're a liar, and that is a hard seed to swallow and especially for a young person or child. I remember the men who molested and raped me, would tell me that nobody would believe me if I told. When I finally opened my mouth my greatest fear came to pass…they didn't! {at first}

Many years passed by that a few told me they were sorry for not believing me. It was hard to receive at first because I had to go through this by myself and the healing was something that I had to do alone as well. I shouldn't say alone because I did have God through it all and I will forever be grateful for that.

When you are being honest you are trying to be genuine and sincere about what you have gone through. It would puzzle me why anyone would

# A Saint With A Past

think I would make up something so sickening? I was a loner but I was not seeking attention, I never mentioned any family members name, I had no hidden agenda or motive to gain from this. This happened to me whether people wanted to believe it or not, it happened to me and I had to endure this my whole life, I never thought I could ever be healed, delivered, or have a man love me past my pain....{tears} God is so good to me because He did it and in that order. {smile}

I had something awful happen to me, and I realize the same thing is happening to many women & men around the world and I wanted to help and share my own personal story no more no less. Hurt people, hurt people. But people who have overcome that hurt just want to help others who are still hurting. Be honest it is a courageous step but necessary in your healing process.

The **tenth step** is <u>Rebuild</u>....love this step to rebuild is to construct and fashion. Now one thing I love about God is that when we ask Him to forgive us, He throws that thing into the sea of forgetfulness and He doesn't bring it back again up again, but we do. So I asked God to forgive me for holding on to my past for as long as I did, and He did.

Then I asked God to help me rebuild my life and He gave me Proverbs 14:1 "Every wise woman buildeth her house: but the foolish plucketh it down with her hands". I first started by asking God to give me back my innocence and allow me to make love to my husband as if he was my first. I fasted and consecrated my body and I will tell you this, making love makes so much sense and is so much better when you ask God to bless it.

I than began to ask God to help me rebuild my way of thinking, because I had so much negativity happen in my life, I was a negative person. Everything was woe is me, and God taught me it was never about me. So God taught me how to rebuild my home, I first laid down the right foundation and that foundation is Jesus Christ, and then my goal and desire was to become a virtuous woman {Proverbs 31}. Now this is not for everyone, however these are the steps that God gave me so I am giving

# A Saint With A Past

them to you.

The **eleventh step** is <u>**Testimony.**</u> To testify is to give reverence to the Almighty God and to give an open declaration of evidence and proof. My testimony was that God can and He will heal and make you whole and I was a living testimony because He did it for me, and He is no respector person.

My testimony is what kept me going, every time I testified of the goodness of the Lord, and it wasn't always in a church setting, sometimes I could just be in the kitchen making something to eat and God would allow a flash to go through my mind and remind me Hallelujah of where I came from.

See I don't know what the end looks like but I have a mind made up to go all the way with Jesus. Because He loved me first, He loved me when I didn't love myself, He love me when I did not know how to love myself. And He kept me when I didn't want to be kept. And He rescued me when I didn't want to be saved. He healed my body and my mind. So my heart and soul cries out Hallelujah because He's worthy of my testimony. Never be ashamed of your testimony. It attests to the goodness of Gods mercy in seeing you through the storms.

The **twelfth step** is <u>**Humility**</u> to be humble means to be modest in self-estimation, and submissive. I give God ALL the glory for everything in my life. When you are humble you take no honor in glorifying yourself you always give God the glory and praise due unto His holy name. When you are humble you remember where God brought you from so when you see others going down a familiar path you minister from love and not condemnation, because you remember how God's mercy and grace saw you through. Even writing this book, it all belongs to Him. I didn't know there was a twelve step program until God revealed it to me; I remember a Pastor once told me CaLisha you have a 12 step program inside of you. I remember thinking there's no such thing, but then he asked me," What did God do for you to heal you?"

# A Saint With A Past

My deliverance, and testimony and the anointing to lay hands and heal others all belongs to God. I know without Him none of this would have been possible to do. That's why my motto is **"I will not compromise the Word of God, for God I live and for God I die"** and when you die to self you can't help but be humble. It is because of God's love I am able to minister to others through my testimony.

So when you read this book and if you try these steps do not give CaLisha any glory this is all belongs to God. I just happened to be the instrument that He saw fit to use. If God leads you to truly try these steps, you have to do it with an open heart and open mind. It truly was a faith walk for me.

*Dear Lord thank You for giving me 12 steps to help to release the bondage of sexual abuse to share with the world. My prayer is that whoever reads this book will also get the healing and restoration; they are in need of. I know if you did it for me I know you will do it for them. Whichever way Lord God you want to use me I am available, if I may touch just one...my work is done. I know there are so many books and methods and programs out there and this is the one you gave me and I know for myself that it work and my prayer is that whoever is reading this book will get healed, rather by my own personal 12 steps or by someone else, as long as you get the glory in their healing, it is in Jesus sweet name I pray, AMEN*

# A Saint With A Past

## HE IS MY PROVIDER

**Philippians 4:19**
*But my God shall supply all your need according to his riches in glory by Christ Jesus*

There was a time when I was coming up before my mom married my dad, we were very impoverished. There were days we went to bed hungry because we had no food. My mother did the best she knew how trying to raise three kids who biological fathers left her to raise us on her own with no financial support. My testimony is not to embarrass my mother but to commend her for the many times she wanted to throw in the towel and give up but didn't. She was not saved at the time.

We had shuffled to at least 15 different apartments by the time I was 9 years old and prior to my mother meeting and marrying my dad who at the time was in the Army. My mom didn't have much money so she would try to scrape up enough money to pay for an apartment for the month and we eventually would get evicted. One of my saddest memories was coming home from school and finding all of our belongings on the sidewalk with people mustering through our things, my mother would tell us to take only what we could carry and we would wind up at a hotel or at my grandmother's house. Now that I am older I have a greater appreciation for my mother who long suffered, endured, and persevered with all three of her children. No matter how tough it got she kept all her children together.

I'll never forget our last apartment 8839 Norton Street in El Paso Texas. That was the apartment that my mother met my dad. My dad did not have any children of his own, and this was his first marriage and to God be the glory for him being a Provider. He sent us my dad. My dad has always taking care of us from day one, we were able to say goodbye to the days of being evicted, we never went hungry again, and we always had hot water, the small things that we sometimes take for granted.

# A Saint With A Past

God has been providing for me ever since I can remember. He knew what was going to happen in my life, and that is why He allowed my grandmother to plant the seed of Christ in me at an early age. Jesus has truly been my Provider and has and still is showing me that no one can provide for me like He can. See we all have an idea of what we want; but only God truly knows what we need. That's why I am so careful when asking God for things, because I know His word says He will give us the desire of our hearts. However I **only** want what **He desires** for me to have.

I want to encourage someone who had a rough childhood, maybe it was even worse off than mine…know this friend. God can and He will restore and give back to you everything that the canker worm stole. I truly believe when you seek God and His righteousness everything else will be added to you if you are seeking Him in the right Spirit and for the right things. I am not telling you what I heard I am telling you what I know, I have tried Him for myself He is the Great I Am. I learned a long time ago that poverty is a state of mind, so when I stop saying I was poor and started saying I was rich even if I had not seen it manifest in the natural yet I believed it in the spirit and now I am able to speak it, live it, and bless others in the process.

Jesus provides for us in ways that are foreign to man. Often time's people cannot understand why it's the little things that cause you to find so much joy. When you are without and you come from less than most you appreciate the small things, and you stay humble when the big things come to past. So yes I may take a little more pride in my house than most, and the main reason is because I remember where I come from. Never judge a book by its cover, take the time to read, you would be amazed and some of the things you will discover in others if you allow compassion to flow.

# A Saint With A Past

*Dear Lord*

*Please touch the hearts of the ones reading this right now and permit them to see that you have always made a way out of no way and you provide for your children. Your Word says" You will never leave us nor forsake us" I pray hearts that are heavy lighten after they have a true encounter with you. I thank you Jesus that you are the Father of all Fathers, and your word says if you take care of the birds and trees, surely you will take care of your servants, thank you for the reassurance in your word when life sometimes wants to make us believe different, we praise your most holy name, in Jesus sweet name I pray...AMEN*

# A Saint With A Past

## DIFFERENT PATHS OF PAIN

*Matthew 7:13 & 14*
*Enter ye in at the strait gate: for wide is the gate,*
*and broad is the way, that leadeth to destruction,*
*and many there be which goin thereat.*
*Because strait is the gate, and narrow is the way,*
*which leadeth unto life, and few there be that find it.*

There were so many wrong roads I could have taken when I was in pain. As a child I saw the devastating effects that drugs can have on many of my family members and friends and told myself a long time ago I would never indulge or succumb to that. I saw the effects of alcohol abuse as well, and even though I took a drink occasionally when of age, I bless God for not allowing alcoholism to be another hurdle for me to climb and be delivered from.

Although my time of ignorance in how to take control of my insecurities would often leave me rendering control to my oppressors through skillful deception and manipulation. I was learning that I could control my fate, and what I commit my mind to do no one can take that from me (although the devil tried, he didn't succeed).

Pity party's was a path I often visited and it was so disappointing that no one would show up but me. I had bouts with depression and the woe is me syndrome for so long I finally got tired of hearing myself murmur and complain about things I could not change. You have to make up your mind to fight and stop feeling sorry for yourself, and I did. I had a son to take care of, and although I was a young girl I told myself I never wanted to be in a situation where I was mentally or physically incapable of caring for my baby. For that reason alone drugs was never an alternative or option for me. I witnessed the devastation and paranoia first hand that comes with drugs and alcohol abuse, and refused to surround my child around that kind of carelessness and neglect. My child gave me a reason to live and be responsible, what is yours? Instead of focusing on reasons to feel defeated, focus on those things that promote life.

# A Saint With A Past

Another path I took was promiscuity. Studies show that people who have been raped or molested tend to either become that themselves or become self-destructive in being promiscuous. I confused sex and love at an early age. I thought if a man had sex with me it symbolized that he loved and cared for me. Boy was I wrong about that, can you imagine being so confused that you see sex as an indicator to determine true affection? The sad thing is that those who have had some form of normalcy in their upbringing would question the intelligence of the victim in my case, but when abuse and neglect is the norm for a child subjected to what I have been through, what do you expect when there is no intervention. I wanted to be loved and feel safe to the point that I didn't have any respect for my body. A history of heartache and toxic relationships brought me to the conclusion that my looks and body was a curse because it brought so much grief and confusion in my life. Men always used me and women couldn't stand me.

It was programmed in my head at an early age that being on my back kept a man around and so I was on my back, but I learned it doesn't matter if you're on your back or front a man will treat you however you allow him to, and in my case when you open that door and make it so easy for them, I truly received what I allowed.

I went down the path of being promiscuous and I am so humble and grateful that even in my time of being ignorant and deceived God still kept hands on me. I cry when I think about what my life could have been like had God not been there for me…He saved me from myself. I never received a sexually transmitted disease, Aids was spreading in epidemic numbers, and through my dark period of promiscuity God covered me. If you're reading this and find yourself in the same dilemma, please stop now and ask God to validate your self-worth. Don't be ashamed of your past, God can purge you and make you whole right now; all you have to do is ask Him. He's standing at the door right now knocking, why don't you answer and let Him in.

I know there's a woman or man reading this right now and I want to encourage you to get a relationship with Jesus so you can know your self-

# A Saint With A Past

worth. For so long I listened to the lies that men and boys had told me, that I was ugly, I wasn't good enough, nobody else is going to want me, nobody would ever believe me. They planted a negative seed inside of me and I watered it because I spoke that same death into my spirit. I would say nobody is going to want me, I am unworthy; nobody will ever believe the things I encountered in my life. And for a long time it seemed like it was true.

But God always has a ram in the bush; He created me for my husband Curtis. {Smile} Friend it's a choice, we can either choose the path of God or the path of the enemy. I can tell you the path of God will restore you, heal you, comfort you, build you, and love you. The path of the devil will destroy you.

I no longer wanted to just go through the motions or exist I wanted to live, that's what my husband always says, "live baby the life God wants you to live, you deserve to be happy". God showed me how to really love CaLisha, and trust me I have my moments when I am not being my best, but at the end of the day God created someone beautiful. Because God is God in my life I no longer wonder down the wrong path. I'm following Christ and I walk softer than ever so that I can hear His footsteps and not my own.

*Dear LORD my prayer is that the person who is reading this right now will no longer be wondering down the wrong path & they will humble themselves and allows you to lead and they will follow softly. Often times we feel like we know the answer and we know what's best, and some of us take a longer route to get to where you are. God no matter the path we are on please show each one reading this book right now, that with you all things are possible and in order to truly be your disciple we have to deny our self and pick up our own cross and follow you. We all have made mistakes and have regrets, thank God for Jesus thank you for showing us mercy no matter how many times we go down the wrong path, thank you for showing us patience which we all need to get it right, we give you glory*

# A Saint With A Past

*and honor that is due unto your holy name in Jesus sweet name I pray, AMEN.*

# A Saint With A Past

## MY BACK IS STRONG ENOUGH

### Galatians 6:5
*For every man shall bear his own burden*

When I began to write about this topic my mind immediately went to the scripture "God will not put more on us than we can bear". But if you don't know the will of God for your life you will never know how much you can really take. I realize now that a lot of things we go through in life are not always brought on by man, the devil or even God. Often times we are the reason for a lot of the issues we face and bring a lot unwanted issues our way based on our own actions.

Even while writing this book I found myself sometimes going up against the devil; and then often times I was going up against myself. I say it all the time we give the devil way to much credit, yet at times we underestimate him as well. God is teaching me to know when CaLisha is in her own way.

For me my late grandmother said I've always had an "old soul" and even till this day I can honestly say she is right. I was deprived of a childhood and had to grow up fast, way before I became a mother. When I was eleven years old, I remember while stationed in Germany, my dad who at the time was in the Army, called me into the kitchen and showed me how to cut up a whole chicken, clean it and cook it.

Later on he took me down stairs in the basement (and for those who have never stayed in military housing in Germany, the basement was where everyone in the building could go to have extra storage and also washers and dryers available) my dad took me down there and showed me how to wash my clothes. I remember it like it was yesterday, he say, "first you fill the water up in the machine, and depending upon what you're washing will determine your water temperature. Then you add the washing detergent. While the machine is filling up with water you separate your clothes; there was a white pile for my whites, a color pile for my colors, a jean pile for my jeans and he said to always wash reds, pinks, and

# A Saint With A Past

oranges together, never with anything because they sometimes bleed. I can honestly say even to this day I still wash my clothes like my dad taught me. I remember that day in the basement my dad said to me, "I can't teach you how to be a woman, but when you grow up a man will never leave you because of the way you cook or keep house". When I think back on that I often wonder, "God was already preparing me for the life that was going to be ahead of me.

My childhood friend Tamika, her mom is definitely a second mom; I call her Mama Boyd {smile}. Mama Boyd already had three kids of her own, yet she took me in. I literally would be at their house all the time. When Christmas would come there was always a gift under the tree for myself and DeVante'. I am sure there were times when her own natural children felt jealous of the attention their mother was given me. What they didn't know was that I really needed her at that time in my life. I remember I was 19 and she came over to my apartment and Tamika and I was there and had gone out to a club the night before, and we had literally brought the party back to my house. Well when Mama Boyd came she saw people in my house, men in my kitchen cooking food that was supposed to be for me and my son. Mama Boyd pulled me aside and told me I needed to really get a relationship with God so I could understand my self-worth. I had never had anyone even tell me I had self-worth because I always felt I wasn't worth anything {especially with my past}. So I thank you Mama Boyd for planting that seed in me way back then.

The devil should have killed me when he thought he had me, now that I am with the Father I know my purpose, position, and place and although the devil tried to destroy me God rebuild me and I will not wavier because I know what God has called me to be. God made my back strong enough to bare everything the enemy threw my way God considered me like he considered Job.

Was I ready for what I was about to go up against? No I was not ready a child out of wedlock, a baby having a baby. Yet I took responsibility and became a young woman and mother at an early age, I did not abort my baby or have my mother raise my child. I dropped out of school my

# A Saint With A Past

sophomore year and worked full time to take care of my baby. I did not utilize the system; I was young, healthy and able so I worked. Nothing in life has been just given to me; I had to work hard for everything. (I do not knock anyone who decided to go a different route; I am just speaking from my own experience). I went back to school and received my high school diploma when I was 22 years old. I then further my education and put myself through college.

The devil threw many things my way one in particular was "*men*". He always knew my relationship with my mother was fragile. He also knew I didn't have men in my life like brothers, uncles, cousins that protected me. So when I got with men, they knew I was a damaged woman, they would get what they want and leave. Although my childhood was hard it did not break me. That's the message I am trying to reach to so many, we all too some degree can relate to hardship and pain.

Eventually we all have to come to the conclusion that we can't control the cards we were dealt in life, but eventually you're going to have to make a move and play your hand. The beautiful thing is God already knows your hand, and has the answer for you to play the right cards. We don't have to make things no harder than what it has to be. You either learn from the past or you allow it to destroy you. I could have easily become a victim, but I wanted more out of life and I knew God had to have more for me. We have been asking the wrong questions and therefore we have been getting the wrong answers.

No longer do I ask why me Lord. I now say, "Please walk through it with me Lord". What are you teaching me Lord? The more I get in my Word the more I get an understanding that God will not put more on us than we can bear. Yes I had an appalling life a lot of suffering but God also gave me some sunshine it was not always rain. I now know if God brought me to it, He will see me through it, yes sometimes life can be unfair, but we have a God that is "Just"

*Dear Lord, My prayer to the one reading this is to not let them give up, allow them to not only feel your presence, but enter into your rest. Allow*

# A Saint With A Past

*them to not only have an experience with you, but a true relationship, please touch their hearts to show them without you they cannot make it and with you all things are possible. God please minister to their broken hearts and let them know you have all their tears in a bottle. Give them strength as an ox to endure their trials and storms thank you God in advance for answer prayers; it is in Jesus sweet name I pray...AMEN*

# A Saint With A Past

## THERE'S A STORY BEHIND THE GLORY

### Isaiah 43:2
*When thou passest through the waters, I will be with thee; and through the rivers, they shall not overflow thee: when thou walkest through the fire, thou shalt not be burned; neither shall the flame kindle upon thee*

I believe we all come to instances in our lives where we wonder why it seems like God has left us. The beautiful thing about having a relationship with God is that it is solely on a trust and faith bases out of a personal relationship with Him. During the difficult times of overcoming hurts we often don't feel God's presence because of our rested pain. Doesn't mean He isn't there, but often times we allow the pain of our circumstances to become bigger than God. Is there anything too hard for God? Is there not a way of escape from the clutches of the pain that plagues you in God? Is there really no hope for you that speaks life and encourages you to live and not die? I tell you that when God gave me a reason to lift up my hung down head I knew I was delivered. It resonated in my walk, it resonated in my talk. God had done a complete makeover over my person and it felt good to feel good.

I knew that the positive change in my inner person would bring about an obvious change in my outer confidence, proven by the different reactions I began to receive from people. People not knowing the battles I was addressing on a daily basis to keep from losing my mind, and to just feel good about myself. I wasn't trying to be conceited, or cute, just confident and strong. I was encouraging myself, not trying to impress nobody, but whether in church, in the work place, or among those who knew me way back then, I'm now being asked "Why do you walk the way you do". Can you believe that? They weren't asking in a curious way, they felt the need to mock me and ridicule me because I was being transformed and renewed in confidence. I couldn't understand for the life of me why anyone would take the time to study my walk so carefully, but while they were studying me, they were missing out on where they were supposed to be walking themselves. So many people love to keep you in a state of misery, you know the saying, *"misery loves company"*.

# A Saint With A Past

I answered and said I walk the way I do because there is a crown on my head, you can't see it in the natural you have to look at in the spirit. My walk is not one of conceit or pride, but a walk of authority and victory because I belong to God, and He called me by name, and out of a life of bondage and I walk like I'm free. But if people want to categorize it into some worldly pattern or cliché so be it. See when you are free you stop fighting things that have no relevance.

See when blessings do come your way people think it's easy to get them. I am here to tell you God promotes and demotes not man, and God rains on the just as well as the unjust, He decides not man. You might as well get it in your mind right now that you can't be healed for man; you have to be healed for yourself first.

People see the blessings but they didn't know the hell I was facing sometimes in my own home. No one knew the struggles I was having, or the many nights that I soaked the pillows crying out to God or how many nights I walked the floors. See all this is done in my midnight hours where it's only me and God. So if people have a problem with your step, step harder, if it's your talk, talk more.

God never gave up on me, so in my time of suffering and travail I leaned all the way on God and I trusted Him to see me out. One of the things that I know I do without uncertainty is obey God, and I move when He tells me to. The bible says obedience is better than sacrifice. I have made it my life's choice to obey and submit to God in everything I do.

I pray, preach, and teach the way I do because of God. God saw fit to place the anointing on me and have me operate in it. I therefore don't try to justify myself anymore to what God blesses me with. Prosperity is another word for glory, and I know the reason I have been blessed in prosperity in my life thus far is because I have put God first in all that I do and all that I am. I check in with God before I check in with anyone else.

Life had almost beaten all the good out of me. But I felt like Job where God allowed the devil to touch him every area, but his soul. I couldn't

# A Saint With A Past

understand why I didn't have a healthy relationship with my mom in the beginning, and so many people would try to give their own explanation as to why not considering the healthy relationship they had with their mother. So for a long time in my life I went down a road of confusion and self-destruction, because I am a mother and I cannot imagine a day going by and my son not know what it feels like to be loved by me. God saw fit to not only loose me from my chains of mental torture I was experiencing; He also healed me in my heart.

God also taught me to not only forgive myself but my mother, she did the best she knew how, and regardless of how I feel she may have handled me she could have given me up, because she had it hard to. See hurt people hurt people and it was a vicious cycle. I myself began to hurt others because I did not know how to love.

We have to stop judging a person because of what we think, take the time to get to know people you would be surprised the road that many have traveled and what they may be able to help you with. So many people ask me do I have regrets in my life. I can honestly say "no" I trust God that He has equipped me to go through and I make sure that's what I do go through and not get stuck. I go through and while I am going through the growing pains, I look in the mirror at what God has created. And to many that may not seem like a lot but to a woman who couldn't look at herself for a long time trust me it's a blessing.

I won't apologize for who God has allowed me to be, I won't down play my calling or the prosperity on my life anymore. I will stay at the feet of Christ and remain that vessel He can use. My glory comes from my Father who saw fit to place it on me.

My glory comes from going from church to church and seeing that the church will continue to hurt its wounded. My glory comes from men taking advantage of the temple God has given me and doing so as they please. My glory comes from having a child out of wedlock at 16. My glory comes from being in an abusive relationship where I lost my mind and God recovered it for me. My glory comes from people saying I wouldn't amount to nothing. My glory comes from being rejected and often disrespected,

# A Saint With A Past

when people whisper and tease and call you out your name at work and you hold your head up that's glory.

When I raise my hands in total surrender and admiration unto God and tears stream down my face and I worship God in Spirit and in Truth. I am giving God the glory and honor that is due unto His holy name. I am thanking God for every time I wanted to give up He picked me up. I am in awe with the way He pursued me when I did not know how to love or that I was worthy to be loved. God brings back to my remembrance where He has brought me from and it keeps me leveled and humbled. I give Him all the praise and Glory for He truly is the Writer of my story

*Dear Lord I ask that you continue to show us who you are in our lives and we never take it for granted and we give You all the praise and glory for being God in our story. Teach us Dear Lord to show others compassion and love because we never truly know where someone has been. We all have a story to tell some more painful than others, teach us how to embrace and show love the way you embrace and showed us love for our story, it is in Jesus sweet name I pray, AMEN*

# A Saint With A Past

## A SAINT WITH A PAST

She didn't think she would ever be loved

Little did she know it would come from up above.

Often times she thought she wouldn't make it in life

God made her a tender mother and wife

She sits in silence with her thoughts

Remembering how much the pain it cost

Not having any regrets of her past

She knows that pain does not last

Her story is how to overcome

Running a race that Jesus already won

Learning to take life as it is

And remembering who her Father really is

Pain does not go away

The Bible is fulfilling it is a suffering way

I am a Saint with a Past

Thanking God that trouble does not always last....

# A Saint With A Past

## FINAL WORD

God allowed me to share my personal life which if we stop and think about for a minute, is not easy to do. You mean I have to expose my secrets God? I have to be ready to sit in a seat where I am opening my life to people and at any time they can judge me, critique me, etc. I don't need to give people anymore fuel to start any fires with me. (Can I get a witness). Often times it's your very own testimony that someone needs to hear to help them over. This book it not for judgment if you are doing that you missed the whole purpose. The purpose of this book is that we all fall short of God's glory and yet He still loves us and pursues us, He still gives us another chance to get it right. I have reason to be angry, bitter, and resentful yet Jesus taught me I have reason but no right. I want to reach someone who had given up on life, someone who knows what every season of pain is. I want to minister and witness to the person who heart is so broken they think they will never be healed or made whole. My pain produce ministry and my life taught me how to have compassion. I want to live a life transparent. I am not pleased with a lot of choices I have made one time or another in my life, however it was not unto death and there is a rainbow after every dark cloud. I want to remind the broken hearted God has not forgotten about them. "A Saint with a Past" is a reminder and a testament to where God has brought me from. My prayer is that you will allow this book to minister to your hurt and remind you we really do serve a true and living and all-knowing God. If you allow God to convert your heart over to him, you will live in your latter days. God loves you and so do I. Thank you for blessing me by reading, and sharing my story...

# A Saint With A Past

## MINISTRY INFORMATION

**CCMW** {Christ Controls My Writing}

**Email**: ccmw2015@gmail.com
**Website**: https://www.ccmw.co

Radio Talk Show
**Food for Your Soul**
http://www.blogtalkradio.com/mercy_grace.com

Life Coach/Motivational Speaker

# A Saint With A Past

**Bibliography or References**

**King James Version Holy Bible**

# A Saint With A Past

## ABOUT THE AUTHOR

Evangelist CaLisha White is married to Elder Curtis White, and is a native of El Paso, Texas who at the tender age of 7 dedicated her life to Christ, under the tutelage and Christian example of her late Grandmother Gustava Kelly.

Her strong Christian foundation along with the prayers of a praying Grandmother would allow her the strength at an early age to overcome an onslaught of life experiences such as poverty, sexual abuse, domestic violence, bearing a child at the age of 16 and cervical cancer tried to knock on her door, but she would not answer.

By the grace of God, she continued to believe in the better good in man and trust that God would make a way out of no way. That way would come through the birth of her son, DeVante'. Left with a child to raise at 16, a child herself, she chose not to allow her age to deter her from being a good mother, but instead use it as a motivation to silence those who said she would never amount to anything. She would branch out on her own at age 17, dropping out of high school so she can work to provide for herself and raise her child according to the biblical principles learned from her Grandmother.

A life acquainted with grief was no excuse for her. She rededicated her life back to Christ in 2002. She returned to school to earn her High School Diploma and graduated with honors. She would further her education studies by earning her Associates in Office Administration & General Studies and a Bachelor's degree in Business Management. She is currently enrolled for the fall of 2015 to obtain her Degree in Christian Ministry.

CaLisha White was ordained an Evangelist in 2005, by Bishop Dexter Speller of House of Faith Ministries, in Anchorage, Alaska, meeting all ministerial requirements. In 2005 Evangelist White would answer the call of God to empower hurting women through her life's example by starting a woman's ministry called "Woodsafehaven Ministry. In 2007 Evangelist

# A Saint With A Past

White would publish her first of many books titled "The Silent Cry Within, The Untold Story" earning her international exposure. A radio talk show would also take shape in 2007 called "Food for Your Soul" where Evangelist White shares sermons from heaven.

God has blessed Evangelist White to go unto another level as He has allowed her to birth {CCMW} Christ Controls My Writing which is the umbrella for "Holiness is Right Ministry". A Magazine entitled "In His Presence" The Tabernacle Experience, stay tuned for "You Don't Know the Cost of my PRAISE" to be released in the fall of 2015. Evangelist White today continues to be a virtuous woman, life coach, motivational speaker, mentor, & servant of God and lover of God in spite of it all!

# A Saint With A Past

## *PERSONAL NOTES*

# A Saint With A Past

# A Saint With A Past

# A Saint With A Past

www.ingramcontent.com/pod-product-compliance
Lightning Source LLC
Chambersburg PA
CBHW071756040426
42446CB00012B/2584